Carol Allan began to write poetry after two divorces and the suicide of her father when she was twenty-seven. As well as being deaf she suffers from dyslexia and dyspraxia, but has found her membership of Rooftop Writers to be an enormous help in her own development as a poet and short story writer.

First Edition 2018

All rights reserved. No part of this publication may be reproduced, stored in a retrieval system or recorded by any means without prior written permission from the publisher. The right of Carol Allan to be identified as the author of this work has been asserted by her in accordance with the Copyright, Designs and Patents Act 1988.

© Carol Allan 2018

ISBN 978-1986127899

A CIP record for this book is available from the British Library

This book is provided subject to the condition that it shall not, by way of trade or otherwise, be lent, re-sold, hired out, or otherwise circulated without the publisher's prior consent in any form of binding or cover other than that in which it is published and without a similar condition including this condition being imposed on the subsequent purchaser.

1 2 3 4 5 6 7 8 9

RAGE!

Carol Allan

4

RAGE!

HOW DARE YOU!

WHO THE HELL DO YOU THINK YOU ARE ?

TEXTING ME OBSCENE TEXTS!

DID YOU THINK THIS WOULD ENAMOUR ME TO YOU?

SHAME ON YOU!

I AM A STRONG WARRIOR WOMAN!

YOU HAVE FUCKED WITH THE WRONG WOMAN!

I SAID NO!

LEAVE ME ALONE!

I PITY YOU AND FEEL SORRY FOR YOU

AND I REALISE

ALL MEN DON'T

ACT LIKE THIS !

IN THE MEANWHILE

I AM A STRONG WARRIOR WOMAN

LOOKING FOR A STRONG WARRIOR MAN

AS EQUALS

6

Thoughts

Thirty lashes o' the cat o'nine tails
Pain, what pain?
Is it only a figment of my imagination?
My dreams my god what dream, dreams
And yet here we are in the midst of chaos
My mindset argues
Crazy, mad, loopy,
Nah! Am sure as hell saner than the next person
Until the next time...

8

Make Love to My Mind

Make love to my mind
Caress my unconscious
Stroke my intellect
Show me your genius
Give me a climax I won't forget
Taste my pearl of wisdom
Plant kisses on my perception
Leave my senses blind
Touch me in the places
You can't reach with fingertips
Make love to my imagination
I'll kiss your thoughts
Without using my lips
And there you go again
Caressing all my senses

10

Love

Our eyes meet

My heart skips a beat,

To embrace this uniqueness

Called love

Calmness of breath

Ultra thin slices of guilt,

Condensed with fears,

You cannot face

The power of love,

All consuming, passionate

Fierce

Deep in my soul,

An ocean across the breeze,

Deep breaths are like little love notes,

For your body

12

Hunk

He is six foot two
And no shades of blue,
Tall dark handsome
Awesome lavishness of a man,
Your voice, my heart skips a beat,
No mean feat,
Chemistry is you touching my mind
And its setting my body on fire,
The touch of your hand, your kiss,
Body so close to mine
Sending shivers down my spine

14

Marriage

Your marriage is broken,
What can you do?
Domestic abuse,
He never hit me,
But silence is like a cancer spread,
The look, god, the look,
What's for tea? is all he'll say,
The atmosphere cuts like a knife, in my heart,
Though the knife is invisible,
You still feel it in every twist and turn,
You make the tea
All the while feeling sick
Tea over you get marks out of ten,
No joke!
And your not even on Master Chef!
You read a book go online,
Anything to distract you from the mental abuse
Of the person you love not speaking to you
Giving you the silent treatment
And then you go to bed
Dying, crying inside,
All the while thinking
What have you done,
Tomorrow things will get better,
But tomorrow never comes

As you realise,

Self preservation comes first
And you leave your broken marriage behind

Pandora's Box

When you open Pandora's Box

It can never be undone,

Your family are shocked

That you don't fit in

To their ideal of what they think you should be,

It's you, they cry, not us,

We don't understand you,

Shock, horror, dismay

How could you do this to me?

Or is this just my perception of what you thought things would be?

You say how can we resolve this?

No idea, sometimes you have to agree to disagree

All because you dared

To open Pandora's Box.

18

Love

Our eyes meet

My heart skips a beat

To embrace this uniqueness called love

Calmness of breath

Ultra thin slices of guilt,

Condensed with fears,

You cannot face

The power of love, all consuming, passionate, fierce

Deep in my soul, An ocean across the breeze,

Deep breaths are like little love notes for your body.

20

Endorphins

Endorphins
You catch them in a jar
Dark mysterious
Agony ecstasy
Sex on legs
Sex on fire
You need this hit
Fusion of the mind
How can you resist
Kissing legs arms, entwined
All because of these damned endorphins.

Single

Sex, divorced,

Still feel horny

This gut retching feeling between my thighs,

Makes me feel alive

Even on my ownsome

Don't feel lonesome

I am a woman of highly charged sexuality

And no, I am not desperate!!

I am a human being with feelings emotions

Happy, sad, joyful,

Glint in my eye, and no it's not a sty!

Miss the closeness of a hug and I am not being smug.

24

Magic Kisses

Magic kisses,

Magic kisses,

So delicious,

His touch his smile, virile, sexy, sophisticated,

Tall dark handsome,

His smell skin upon skin

The smell of his aftershave,

Sends me all giddy

What does he see? When he looks at me?

A woman oozing sexuality.

26

Bosses

Psychotic bosses
Cut their losses
They never give a toss
At your loss,
Cause they're the boss, and boy don't you know it,
If only they showed
Feeling, compassion
But that's not there reaction!
Narcissus is just taking the piss!

28

Totally

Totally smash it!

Totally scunnered!

Totally gobsmacked!

Totally awesome!

Totally fucked!

Totally fab friends!

Totally worth it!

Totally in five!

Totally humdrum!

Totally what!

The word is...

Totally!

30

Brave the Shave

Brave the shave
Early to your grave?
Nah' it's a worthwhile cause
That stops you to pause
Reflect, inspect, inject,
A life worthwhile,
All for cancer research
To find a cure,
To be whole and pure
To be back to your old self
And not left on the shelf
Whatever that might be
To have a cup of tea
Wherever that might be.

32

Chocolate and Coffee

Chocolate and coffee,

A marriage made in heaven

Which one tastes better?

Of course, chocolate they say,

It's smooth dark sexy

Illuminating, hardcore,

But then so is coffee

Dark rich calling you

With it's instant hit

And aroma

Like someone on a mission

You need a hit of chocolate coffee both at the same time

To get you through the day night

So you can instantly feel alive!

Craving this chocolate coffee.

34

RAPE IN A MARRIAGE

SEPTEMBER 2006

YES, YOU, MY HUSBAND, RAPED ME!

WE WERE ON HOLIDAY IN ROME

THE ROMANTIC CITY OF ROME

FOR ME THERE WAS NO ROMANCE

WE DID GO TO BED

I SAID NO TO YOU!

SURE WE BOTH HAD BEEN DRINKING, NOT MUCH,

YOU OBVIOUSLY NEVER HEARD A WORD I SAID,

YET AGAIN I SAID NO!

GO ON, YOU SAID, WE BOTH WANT TO!

I SAID NO!

YOU WERE SO MUCH STRONGER THAN ME

SO IN REALITY

WHAT COULD I DO

WHY DOES NO ONE LISTEN WHEN YOU SAY NO!

A Wet Dream

Do men have wet dreams

How about women?

To wake up moist between your legs,

To turn over and to touch your balls,

To feel your erection

Getting bigger and bigger?

Then to turn you on your back and to start kissing your stomach then to lick and caress your penis,

To hear you softly, moan and gasp, as I lick up and down the shaft of your penis

All the while trying to take things slow,

As I want to jump on you

And feel you Inside me

As I want you to come slow, sure, then quick arching moaning till we both can't take anymore and climax together, then fall back exhausted in our love-making cuddling in together (missing the wet patch)

And then yikes!! I wake up alone and realise its a dream.

My Father

Dad, why did you have to go,

To leave me, my brother, mum,

Thirty years might have passed

Sometimes I think I am still in shock from it all

For you to feel so low

And to take your own life

Depression is a terrible thing

I still love you, Dad, miss you,

Think of you every day

And yet when I feel in the depths of despair

I say no to myself

As everyday is a gift

And even though there have been some dark days

I still have wonderful memories of you, Dad,

Your laugh, your smile

Your dry sense of humour

And above all, Dad, I cherish you in my heart.

Shape

When I think of her-him

All that comes to mind is a poem, made of just a few truthful words, whispered by someone in love,

Hundreds of years ago, unable to perceive the shape of you,

I find you all around me.

Your presence fills your eyes with your love.

It humbles my heart, for you are everywhere.

42

Heart

Why does the pain in my heart not stop my heart beating?

The wonderest sound of the rain going pitter-pater on the window pain,

Of my human existence of this process we call life!

AHA!

Well I am alive with the wonderful sound of my heart beating,

Heart be still no more, and hone into the sights, sounds

Of nature, the wind howling, the sun shining, the birds singing

In all their morning glory,

To taste the very essence of this thing we call life

And to grab it by the balls

As if our very life depended on it,

Well fuck it, I am grabbing life by the balls,

Nae' mair holding on by the shirt tails,

I am going to touch, see, feel, express, laugh, cry, shout, dance,

Sing to my hearts content even through

I am terrified, excited,

Horrified to go one step forward and not two steps back

In this wonderful human existence we call life!

44

If you have been adversely affected by any of the poems
in this book please contact
Forth Valley Rape Crisis Centre

01786 439244
support@forthvalleyrapecrisis.org.uk

46

94841375R00026

Made in the USA
Columbia, SC
03 May 2018